SOME MAJOR EVENTS IN WORLD WAR II

THE EUROPEAN THEATER

1939 SEPTEMBER—Germany invades Poland; Great Britain, France, Australia, & New Zealand declare war on Germany; Battle of the Atlantic begins. NOVEMBER—Russia invades Finland.

1940 APRIL—Germany invades Denmark & Norway. MAY—Germany invades Belgium, Luxembourg, & The Netherlands; British forces retreat to Dunkirk and escape to England. JUNE—Italy declares war on Britain & France; France surrenders to Germany. JULY—Battle of Britain begins. SEPTEMBER—Italy invades Egypt; Germany, Italy, & Japan form the Axis countries. OCTOBER—Italy invades Greece. NOVEMBER—Battle of Britain over. DECEMBER—Britain attacks Italy in North Africa.

1941 JANUARY—Allies take Tobruk. FEBRUARY—Rommel arrives at Tripoli. APRIL—Germany invades Greece & Yugoslavia. JUNE—Allies are in Syria; Germany invades Russia. JULY—Russia joins Allies. AUGUST—Germans capture Kiev. OCTOBER—Germany reaches Moscow. DECEMBER—Germans retreat from Moscow; Japan attacks Pearl Harbor; United States enters war against Axis nations.

1942 MAY—first British bomber attack on Cologne. JUNE—Germans take Tobruk. SEPTEMBER—Battle of Stalingrad begins. OCTOBER—Battle of El Alamein begins. NOVEMBER—Allies recapture Tobruk; Russians counterattack at Stalingrad.

1943 JANUARY—Allies take Tripoli. FEBRUARY—German troops at Stalingrad surrender. APRIL—revolt of Warsaw Ghetto Jews begins. MAY—German and Italian resistance in North Africa is over; their troops surrender in Tunisia; Warsaw Ghetto revolt is put down by Germany. JULY—allies invade Sicily; Mussolini put in prison. SEPTEMBER—Allies land in Italy; Italians surrender; Germans occupy Rome; Mussolini rescued by Germany. OCTOBER—Allies capture Naples; Italy declares war on Germany. NOVEMBER—Russians recapture Kiev.

1944 JANUARY—Allies land at Anzio. JUNE—Rome falls to Allies; Allies land in Normandy (D-Day). JULY—assassination attempt on Hitler fails. AUGUST—Allies land in southern France. SEPTEMBER—Brussels freed. OCTOBER—Athens liberated. DECEMBER—Battle of the Bulge.

1945 JANUARY—Russians free Warsaw. FEBRUARY—Dresden bombed. APRIL—Americans take Belsen and Buchenwald concentration camps; Russians free Vienna; Russians take over Berlin; Mussolini killed; Hitler commits suicide. MAY—Germany surrenders; Goering captured.

THE PACIFIC THEATER

1940 SEPTEMBER—Japan joins Axis nations Germany & Italy.

1941 APRIL—Russia & Japan sign neutrality pact. DECEMBER—Japanese launch attacks against Pearl Harbor, Hong Kong, the Philippines, & Malaya; United States and Allied nations declare war on Japan; China declares war on Japan, Germany, & Italy; Japan takes over Guam, Wake Island, & Hong Kong; Japan attacks Burma.

1942 JANUARY—Japan takes over Manila; Japan invades Dutch East Indies. FEBRUARY—Japan takes over Singapore; Battle of the Java Sea. APRIL—Japanese overrun Bataan. MAY—Japan takes Mandalay; Allied forces in Philippines surrender to Japan; Japan takes Corregidor; Battle of the Coral Sea. JUNE—Battle of Midway; Japan occupies Aleutian Islands. AUGUST—United States invades Guadalcanal in the Solomon Islands.

1943 FEBRUARY—Guadalcanal taken by U.S. Marines. MARCH—Japanese begin to retreat in China. APRIL—Yamamoto shot down by U.S. Air Force. MAY—U.S. troops take Aleutian Islands back from Japan. JUNE—Allied troops land in New Guinea. NOVEMBER—U.S. Marines invade Bougainville & Tarawa.

1944 FEBRUARY—Truk liberated. JUNE—Saipan attacked by United States. JULY—battle for Guam begins. OCTOBER—U.S. troops invade Philippines; Battle of Leyte Gulf won by Allies.

1945 JANUARY—Luzon taken; Burma Road won back. MARCH—Iwo Jima freed. APRIL—Okinawa attacked by U.S. troops; President Franklin Roosevelt dies; Harry S. Truman becomes president. JUNE—United States takes Okinawa. AUGUST—atomic bomb dropped on Hiroshima; Russia declares war on Japan; atomic bomb dropped on Nagasaki. SEPTEMBER—Japan surrenders.

WORLD AT WAR

Prisoners of War

WORLD AT WAR

Prisoners of War

By R. Conrad Stein

Consultant:
Professor Robert L. Messer, Ph.D.
Department of History
University of Illinois, Chicago

CHILDRENS PRESS ®
CHICAGO

A Japanese soldier with bayonet stands guard as exhausted American soldiers stop for a moment of rest during the infamous Bataan Death March.

Library of Congress Cataloging-in-Publication Data

Stein, R. Conrad.
  Prisoners of war.

  (World at war)
  Includes index.
  Summary: Describes the various treatment, from relatively civil to unbearable, given to both military and civilian prisoners of war during World War II.
  1. World War, 1939-1945—Prisoners and prisons—Juvenile literature.   [1. World War 1939-1945—Prisoners and prisons]   I. Title. II. Series.
D805.A2S73   1987   940.54′72   86-34291
ISBN 0-516-04799-X

FRONTISPIECE:
Having just surrendered to Allied forces, battle-weary German soldiers await transfer to a prisoner-of-war camp.

PICTURE CREDITS:
UPI: Cover, pages 4, 6, 8, 9, 10, 11, 12 (left), 13, 17, 18, 28, 36, 37, 42, 44, 46
WIDE WORLD: Pages 12 (right), 15, 19, 35, 38, 39, 40, 41, 43, 45
AMERICAN RED CROSS: Pages 20, 21, 24, 27
© R.W. KIMBALL, COURTESY AIR FORCE MUSEUM, DAYTON, OHIO: Pages 23, 25, 26, 29, 31, 32, 33, 34

COVER PHOTO:
Allied soldiers imprisoned in a German camp in France stare with dazed expressions at the American troops who have come to liberate them.

PROJECT EDITOR:
Joan Downing

CREATIVE DIRECTOR:
Margrit Fiddle

On April 9, 1942, the sun rose over a string of white flags in the war-scarred Philippine jungle. Months earlier, American and Filipino troops had dug in on the Bataan Peninsula to stage a last-ditch fight against the Japanese invaders. The soldiers battled bravely, but they were cut off from supplies. All units were low on ammunition, and there was so little food that some of the men were reduced to eating rats. Surrender was their only choice. Seventy-five thousand weary troops lay down their rifles and climbed out of their trenches. It marked the greatest defeat ever suffered by United States Army forces.

Japanese General Masaharu Homma was unable to feed or provide transport for so many prisoners. He ordered them to march sixty-five miles over jungle trails to a rail junction at Camp O'Donnell. The grueling trek took six days under a blistering tropical sun. Many of the Americans and Filipinos suffered from malaria or dysentery. Some seven thousand soldiers died along the side of the road, succumbing to starvation and disease.

Near the end of the brutal march, prisoners used improvised stretchers to carry comrades who had collapsed along the way.

Many who trudged on were kicked or beaten along the way, and those who collapsed from exhaustion were shot and killed by their Japanese guards. Newspapers in the United States called this ordeal the "Bataan Death March."

American Colonel William Dyess survived the death march and described the cold-blooded shootings: "As members of the murder squad stooped over each huddled form, there would be an orange flash in the darkness and a sharp [gun] report. The bodies were left where they lay, that other prisoners coming behind us might see them . . . Eventually one [Japanese guard] who spoke English asked, 'Sleepy? You want sleep? Just lie down on the road. You get good, long sleep.'"

About seven thousand American and Filipino soldiers died during the sixty-five-mile trek. Some succumbed to starvation or disease; others were shot or beaten to death by Japanese guards.

In the midst of this brutality, however, a few Americans reported receiving kind treatment. Some Japanese guards shared their food with the half-starved prisoners. A Japanese tank officer ran up to one marching American and embraced him. They had been classmates at UCLA. At the start of the march, those judged to be severely wounded or wasted by disease were transported to Camp O'Donnell on the few trucks Japanese General Homma had at his service. Yet there was no pattern to the treatment the prisoners received. One section of the long line of men would be supervised by a humane Japanese officer, while a mile to the rear marched a brute who prodded the captives with bayonets and shot stragglers.

These newly captured German soldiers, who were among the more than fifteen million men and women taken prisoner during World War II, had no way of knowing what kind of treatment they would receive from their captors.

German prisoners file through the barbed-wire-enclosed stockade
of a POW camp in England.

This uneven treatment mirrored the lives of
most prisoners of war (POWs) in World War II. A
POW's existence ran the gamut from unbearable
cruelty, to confinement that was cursed with
boredom and poor food, to a lifestyle that
approached comfort. Men and women captured
during the war faced a grim "lottery." This lottery
was influenced by the POW's nationality, skin
color, military rank, and, especially, the character
of his or her captors. For example, although
anyone taken prisoner by the Japanese was bound
to suffer, white POWs suffered less than Asians.

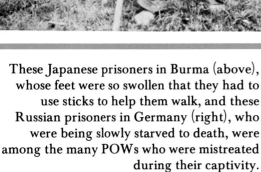

These Japanese prisoners in Burma (above), whose feet were so swollen that they had to use sticks to help them walk, and these Russian prisoners in Germany (right), who were being slowly starved to death, were among the many POWs who were mistreated during their captivity.

The lottery had many strange quirks. The Germans treated French, British, and American POWs properly, but were brutal in their dealings with Russians. The Russians were equally severe in their treatment of German POWs. Both countries abused Polish prisoners. "Winners" of the lottery were the Germans and Italians captured by the American and British armies.

German officers on their way to a POW camp in England receive sandwiches from their British captors.

In theory, certain rules governed the treatment of POWs. In 1929, the last of a series of meetings called the Geneva Convention was held in Switzerland. The Geneva Convention decreed that prisoners in future wars must be guaranteed certain rights, including medical care, proper food, and mail from home. The convention also called for neutral governments and agencies to inspect POW camps. During World War II, the Swiss government and the International Red Cross kept a check on European POW camps. The Soviet Union, however, never signed the Geneva agreement, and the government of Japan never ratified it. Those two powers processed millions of prisoners during the war years.

Despite many acts of individual kindness, the Japanese were generally cruel to their prisoners. An ancient Japanese military code of honor called *Bushido* demanded that all soldiers fight to their last breath and never even think of giving up. Consequently, Japanese guards—who were soldiers first—looked upon prisoners as cowards and treated them accordingly.

When the garrison at Singapore fell in 1942, some sixty-one thousand British, Dutch, and Australian soldiers surrendered to the Japanese army. Several months later they were put to work building a 260-mile railroad that ran from Burma to Thailand. Its route climbed over mountains, cut through dense jungle, and bridged dozens of streams and rivers. The novel and movie *The Bridge On the River Kwai* told the grim story of building a bridge for this railroad. To the Japanese, the railroad was to be a lifeline for their vast new empire. For the Allied slave laborers, it became "Death Railway."

These American prisoners show the effects of the meager diet provided at Japanese prison camps.

The Geneva Convention stipulated that only low-ranking enlisted POWs could be put to work, and only on non-military projects. The Japanese, however, forced everyone to work on the railroad construction. A prisoner who claimed to be too sick to work was given no food. If his work pace slackened, a guard would beat him with bamboo sticks. The POWs had to toil sixteen-hour shifts and were given only a few handfuls of rice to eat a day. The work continued for almost a year and a half. At least sixteen thousand Allied POWs died from exhaustion, disease, and undernourishment.

As the Japanese overran European and American outposts in Asia, they captured thousands of civilian men, women, and children. These non-combatants were forced to live in the same kinds of barbed-wire-enclosed compounds as were the soldiers taken prisoner. Generally, though, the Japanese allowed the civilians a greater degree of freedom. The captives ran their own schools and churches, and even circulated camp newspapers. A Dutch boy named Hendrik Leffelaar, whose family was imprisoned in an Asian camp, wrote in his diary: "July 10, 1944: Got report cards today; fortunately promoted to 10th grade. My grades aren't so hot." While this sounds like an innocent note from a schoolboy, the Dutch civilian prisoners suffered from a wretched diet, poor medical care, and ravaging jungle diseases. Hendrik Leffelaar's very next entry read, "July 11, 1944: School friends and members of his old Boy Scout troop said a last farewell to Hanns Wildberg. Hanns died suddenly. Typhoid."

Above: This overcrowded gymnasium served as
the living quarters for civilian prisoners at
Santo Tomas, a Japanese internment camp in the
Philippines.
Left: A civilian prisoner at Santo Tomas cooks
her children's daily meal of cornmeal mush.
Below: American prisoners at Bilibid prison
camp in the Philippines serve watery soup to
fellow inmates.

Two French prisoners work while being watched by German soldiers.

American and western-European POWs held in German camps fared better. For the most part, the Germans abided by the rules of the Geneva Convention, with several grave exceptions. They denied proper food to their war prisoners. And the concentration camps that held their political prisoners and slave laborers were among the worst examples of inhumanity in the history of warfare. Still, American and British prisoners were allowed regular mail, and they were paid for the labor they were forced to perform. Also, as a rule, German authorities did not disturb the precious food

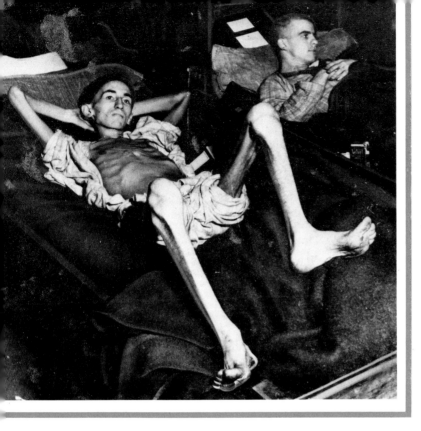

This emaciated American prisoner survived a German POW camp on a daily ration of a slice of bread and a bowl of soup made of dried peas and peeled potatoes.

parcels that were shipped in from the outside. However, exceptions did become more frequent as the war devastated Germany and its supply lines became disrupted.

Typically, the Germans served their captives a slice of bread and a watery soup made from tiny bits of potatoes and cabbage. The bread was likely to be moldy. "Never during my captivity did I get enough to eat," said one American POW. Others claimed that the constant feeling of hunger was maddening. They could think of nothing but food. Some POWs lost up to eighty pounds.

A warehouse in Geneva, Switzerland filled with Red Cross packages intended for Allied POWs in Europe

Red Cross food parcels were the POW's lifeline. The parcels were shoebox-sized packages containing cheese, canned meat and fish, dried fruit, cigarettes, and soap. They were paid for by the American and British governments, and were delivered through neutral countries to Geneva, Switzerland. From there they were distributed to camps by the International Red Cross. By the end of the war, the American Red Cross had sent more than two hundred thousand tons of packages —enough to form a line stretching from Chicago to Berlin. To this day, most Allied POWs insist that they would have starved to death had it not been for the Red Cross packages.

Contents of a typical American Red Cross food parcel

Labels in image: Corned Beef, CORNED BEEF, Powdered Milk, Oleomargarine, Cigarettes, Pork Luncheon Meat, Biscuits, Raisins, Salmon, Cheese, American PROCESS CHEESE, Liver Paste, SEEDLESS RAISINS, Fresno, California, Soap, Orange Concentrate, Coffee, Sugar, Cane Sugar, Dots, Chocolate

Every American and British prisoner in Europe received one food parcel a week. Despite their growling hunger, POWs never wolfed down their rations on the first day. Instead, they squirreled their precious food away and ate it bit by bit in order to make it last until the next parcel delivery. When deliveries were delayed, a cloud of gloom shrouded the camp. Often, parcel items were used for trade. During the war years, soldiers on all sides smoked cigarettes. German guards were fond of American cigarettes, and bartered fruit and bread for them. Such trade took place in secret because the guards would be severely punished if caught by the camp commander.

Aside from hunger pangs, boredom plagued the POWs. Long hours of idleness in overcrowded barracks led to a certain form of madness the Americans called "going wire-happy." It was so named for the ever-present strings of barbed wire that cut the POW off from the outside world. Signs of being wire-happy included ranting and raving, picking fights with other camp inmates, and huddling in a corner muttering to oneself. Suicide among wire-happy POWs was common.

The cry "Mail call!" signaled the highlight of a POW's life. Even the most trifling letter was read and reread a hundred times. But the prisoner who failed to get a letter, or who received bad news from home, felt an overpowering sense of despair and helplessness. Prisoners' mail was routed through neutral countries. The Geneva Convention required all warring nations to submit a list of their captives so that relatives would know their loved ones were alive and could receive letters. Germany allowed letters to pass freely, but Japan interfered with its captives' mail. In four

An accordian could be used to conceal a forbidden radio set.

years, American General Jonathan Wainwright's wife wrote him three hundred letters. He received only six.

The POW hungered for news from the fighting fronts. Radios were forbidden because they could be used to aid insurrection. Still, almost every camp in Germany had a radio hidden away— under the floorboards, in a hollowed-out book, or inside a guitar or accordion. British and American agents sometimes placed tiny radio parts inside Red Cross packages, to be put together by skilled craftsmen in the barracks. News bulletins from the British Broadcasting Company (BBC) monitored the progress of Allied armies through Europe. The POWs then drew lines on secret maps and tried to estimate when their camp would be liberated. The BBC sometimes transmitted personal messages, such as news of marriages and births in the families of POWs.

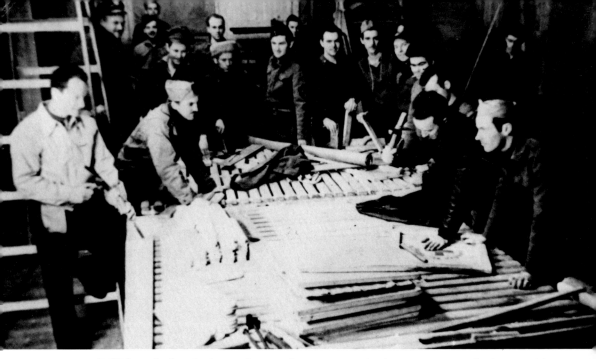

POWs at Stalag Luft 3 in Sagan, Germany used whatever materials they could find, including Red Cross packing crates, to build the sets for their plays.

To relieve their boredom and take their minds off their rumbling bellies, POWs in Germany staged plays and sometimes even lavish musical productions. Generally, the Germans encouraged these performances because they gave the POWs a chance to let off steam and lessened the chances of prisoner rebellion. Often, German guards waited for "opening night" as anxiously as did the compound inmates. The British staged the most elaborate extravaganzas. Some of their musicals featured lines of high-stepping "chorus girls." The "girls" were actually inmates dressed in leggy costumes and sporting mops for wigs.

The elaborate
productions staged
by the prisoners
of Stalag Luft 3
included plays
(above and left)
and variety shows
(below). The
women's parts,
of course, had to
be played by men.

Spending time in the camp library (above), running the camp radio station (right), and participating in sports (below) were some of the things Allied POWs in German camps could do to fill the endless hours.

Some Allied POWs in German camps spent time working on a camp newspaper. The name of this paper is a takeoff on *Stars and Stripes*, the daily newspaper of the United States Armed Forces.

POWs also read books, gambled for cigarettes, and participated in sports. Organized boxing matches brought the whole compound outside to watch. The British played rousing games of soccer, and their German guards stood by applauding superior passes and shots. However, the Germans were thoroughly confused by softball, the favorite game among American POWs. Using books shipped in by various organizations, some camps developed well-stocked libraries. One American captive read all fifty books of the Harvard Classics twice.

Winston Churchill's heroic escape from a prison camp during the Boer War served as an inspiration to British prisoners plotting to escape from German camps.

Despite these diversions, POWs burned to put the barbed wire behind them and go home. Of all the prisoners held in Germany, none were more obsessed with escaping than the British. British escapees hoped first to get beyond the barbed wire, then make their way to France or Belgium and contact the underground resistance, and then find a boat to England. To the English POW, escape became an act of great drama. The theme had dominated British World War I adventure novels and movies. Four decades earlier, Winston Churchill himself had won fame when he broke out of a POW camp in South Africa during the Boer War.

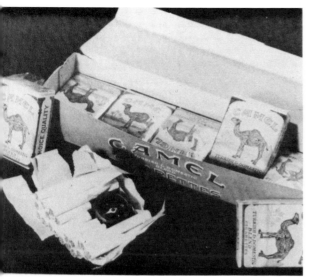

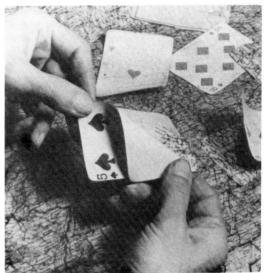

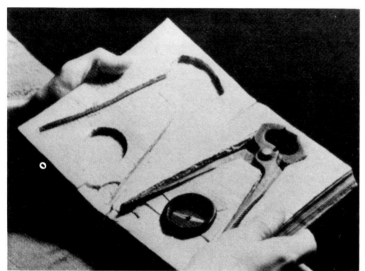

Items intended to help prisoners escape were smuggled into German camps in a number of ways. Compasses and other tools could be hidden inside cigarette packages (above left) or in hollowed-out books (left). Maps printed on very thin paper could be inserted between the layers of playing cards (above).

Few POWs were more determined to escape than British fighter pilot Thomas D. Calnan. Devoting every thought to escape was Calnan's method of staying sane. As he later wrote, "Getting one up [on the Germans] gave me enough personal satisfaction to make my imprisonment bearable for a long time to come."

Several times he tried burrowing under the barbed-wire fence of his camp. During one attempt, his tunnel collapsed on his back, almost burying him alive. On three occasions, Calnan managed to steal his way past the main gate. Once, he strolled out disguised as a Russian laborer. But after each breakout, he was quickly recaptured.

One of the most ingenious prison breakouts was carried out by a group of British prisoners at the huge POW camp near Sagan in Germany. The getaway was inspired by the ancient story of how Greeks invaded the city of Troy by hiding inside a wooden horse. Using discarded Red Cross packing crates, the POWs built the kind of wedge-shaped vaulting horse that is used in gymnasiums. In the spring of 1943, the prisoners carried this vaulting horse to a spot near the barbed-wire fence. Hidden inside were two men clutching tin cans and homemade picks designed for digging. While other prisoners leapfrogged and somersaulted over the horse, the two inside began frantically digging a tunnel. At the end of the

German guards who concentrated on searching out and destroying escape tunnels were known in POW slang as "ferrets."

exercise period, the diggers put a lid on the hole and brushed sand over it. Then, along with bags of the dirt they had scooped up, they remained inside the horse, and were hauled back to the barracks. The next morning the POWs carried the horse to exactly the same spot and the digging process began once more.

It took four tedious months for the prisoners to tunnel beyond the barbed wire. The scheme worked to perfection. At night three men squirmed through the tunnel, and each of them eventually reached England. After the war, a popular British movie, *The Wooden Horse*, glamorized the Trojan Horse Operation.

During the digging of the tunnel at Sagan that was later made famous in the movie *The Great Escape*, fresh air was pumped to workers through a homemade pump (left) attached to a pipeline made out of Red Cross dried-milk tins (above).

Tunneling on an even larger scale took place at another compound at Sagan. With tremendous planning and effort, British POWs scratched out a tunnel that was thirty feet below the ground and ran more than three hundred feet in length. The tunnel was equipped with rails and a rope-drawn trolley designed to pull a man lying on his back. On a March evening in 1944, seventy-six POWs rode the trolley, one by one, to freedom. Paul Brickhill, who helped build the tunnel but stayed behind at the camp, later wrote a thrilling

To keep the Sagan tunnel from caving in, diggers shored its walls with wooden slats taken from prisoners' bed frames. Dug-up soil was hauled back through the tunnel on a trolley (above) and then carried out in bags hidden underneath a prisoner's coat (right).

book about the operation, *The Great Escape*. It was eventually made into a popular movie.

Once beyond the barbed wire, however, escapees emerged in the middle of the Nazi-run police state. Even if they could find civilian clothes to wear, most POWs spoke no German, and none could produce a valid identity card when challenged by police. Generally, escapees were arrested within fifty miles of their compound. One recaptured British officer wrote. "A whole society was against us, and for practical purposes that meant . . . the whole world."

Despite careful planning, most POWs who tried to escape from German camps were quickly recaptured. Two Americans who made an unsuccessful attempt are shown listed in a police bulletin (left) and in handcuffs just after their recapture (right).

When recaptured, POWs were usually sentenced to a term of solitary confinement. But the breakout later written up as *The Great Escape* infuriated Nazi leader Adolf Hitler. He demanded that his special police force, the Gestapo, investigate the matter. Of the seventy-six men who broke out of the compound, only three reached England. The rest were recaptured, and fifty of the men were executed by the Gestapo.

German prisoners being forced to march in freezing weather toward a Russian prison camp

By far the most brutal treatment of prisoners in the European war occurred in the Russian-German conflict. Nazi theory held that Russians were inferior people. Russian dictator Josef Stalin wrote off all war prisoners, even his own. Said Stalin, "There are no Russian prisoners of war. The Russian soldier fights on till death." These attitudes led to the doom of both Russian and German prisoners on the eastern front. The death figures in the prison camps of both sides are shocking. Of the 5.7 million Russian prisoners captured by the Germans, more than half died. The Russians captured 3.5 million Germans, 1.5 million of whom died in Soviet camps.

German POWs playing croquet at Camp Breckenridge in Kentucky

By 1945, more than four hundred thousand Axis POWs were living in camps in the United States. The overwhelming majority of those prisoners were German. Years after the war ended, one German ex-prisoner told an American reporter, "I'll tell you, pal, if there is ever another war, get on the side that America isn't, then get captured by the Americans—you'll have it made."

German prisoners in the United States ate better than most of the civilians in their war-torn homeland.

German POWs in America ate eggs, meat, milk, cheese, fruits, and vegetables every day. These food items were undreamed-of luxuries in war-torn Germany. The Geneva Convention specified that POWs must eat at least as well as their guards, and the United States followed that edict to the letter. Most POW camps were in rural areas, and low-ranking German enlisted men were assigned to work for farmers as field hands. Often they worked and ate side by side with Americans.

German POWs in American camps were free to spend their wages at the camp canteen.

Sometimes the Germans formed lasting friendships with the families they worked for, and kept up a correspondence with them after the war. German POW workers in American camps were paid about eighty cents a day. They were free to save the money until after their release, or spend it at the camp canteens that were manned by fellow inmates.

To help ease the manpower shortage in the United States, Axis POWs were put to work doing everything from cutting down trees (above) to harvesting potatoes (below).

German prisoners receiving mail from home (above) and playing cards in their barracks (below)

German POWs attending a lecture on American democracy

Despite this relatively easy life, a large number of German POWs remained devoted Nazis. The Americans allowed the Germans to greet each other with their traditional "Heil Hitler!" salute, and in some camps pictures of Hitler hung at honored spots on the walls of the barracks. Bands of diehard Nazis operated Gestapo organizations in many compounds. They beat and even murdered fellow Germans who were heard to mutter anti-Nazi statements. After the war, fourteen Nazi ringleaders of a series of prison-camp murders were convicted and hung by American authorities.

Overjoyed Russian prisoners raise aloft one of the American soldiers who have come to liberate them from a camp in Germany.

In the spring of 1945, American tanks approached a prison camp in Moosburg, Germany. Machine-gun fire rattled from the tanks, but no German defenders returned the shots. After a moment of silence, a voice within the camp cried, "It's over. The war's over. We're free." The camp inmates then swarmed out of their compounds. Some cheered, others wept, and still more knelt in prayer. All over Germany, this scene was repeated as Allied troops liberated

Liberated Russian prisoners pour out of a camp near Eselheide, Germany.

prison camps. Several months later, Japanese prison guards simply walked away from POW camps after their government surrendered. At the time of liberation, many prisoners of the Japanese looked like walking skeletons. Yet the joy they felt approached hysteria. Said one POW, "We hovered on the brink of tears and laughter, not daring to give way to either for fear we could not stop."

British soldiers enjoy their first meal as free men after being
liberated from a German camp by the advancing U.S. Ninth Army.

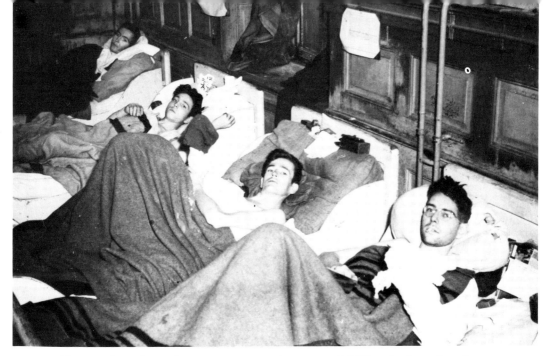

Too weak to show their excitement, American POWs who have just been liberated rest in the ward of a German prison hospital.

It is estimated that at least fifteen million men and women were captured and held prisoner during the years of World War II. Their lives varied from the relative comfort enjoyed by Germans interned in America, to the hell suffered by Russians imprisoned in German camps. Still, for all POWs, life was an empty, demoralizing ordeal. Their despair can be seen in the lines of this poem written by an American held in a German prisoner-of-war camp:

> The unused, empty days crawling slowly by
> Each leave a question burning in the mind —
> How long? A little while? For what?

Three American POWs, each of whom lost a leg after developing gangrenous
jungle sores while imprisoned in the Philippines, are greeted by one of
their American liberators.

Index

Page numbers in boldface type indicate illustrations

Allied prisoners of war, 14-15, 20, **24**, **25**, **26**

American prisoners of war, **6**, 7-9, **8**, **9**, 12, **15**, **17**, 18-24, **19**, **24**, **25**, **26**, 27, 34, 45, **45**, **46**

American Red Cross, 20, **21**

Australian prisoners of war, 14

Axis prisoners of war, 36, **39**

Bataan Death March, **6**, 7-9, **8**, **9**

Bataan Peninsula, 7

Bilibid prison camp, **17**

Boer War, 28

books, in camps, 27

boredom, in camps, 22, 24

Brickhill, Paul, 32-33

The Bridge on the River Kwai, 14

British Broadcasting Company (BBC), 23

British prisoners of war, 12, 14-15, 18-24, 27-34 **32**, **33**, **44**

Burma, 14

Bushido code, 14

Calnan, Thomas D., 29-30

Camp Breckenridge, **36**

Camp O'Donnell, 7, 9

Churchill, Winston, 28, **28**

civilian prisoners, 16, **17**, 18

concentration camps, 18

Dutch prisoners of war, 14

Dyess, William, 8

escape attempts, of Allied POWs, 28-34, **29**, **31**, **32**, **33**, **34**

"ferrets," 31

Filipino prisoners of war, 7-9, **9**

food, in POW camps, 11, 15, **17**, 18-21, **19**, 37, **37**

food parcels for POWs, 18-19, 20-21, **20**, **21**

forced labor, in camps, 14-15, 18, **18**, 37-38, **39**

French prisoners of war, 12, **18**

Geneva Convention, and rights of POWs, 13, 15, 22, 37

German prisoners of war **4**, **10**, **11**, 12, 13, **13**, 35, **35**, 36-38, **36**, **37**, **38**, **39**, 40, 41, **41**, 45

Gestapo, 34

"going wire-happy," 22

The Great Escape, 32, 33, 34

Hitler, Adolf, 34, 41

Homma, Masaharu, 7

inspection of POW camps, 13

International Red Cross, 13, 20, **20**

Italian prisoners of war, 12

Japanese, treatment of POWs, **6**, 7-9, **8**, **9**, 13, 14-16, 22-23

Japanese prisoners of war, **12**

Leffelaar, Hendrik, 16

liberation of Allied POWs, 42-43, **42**, **43**, **44**, **45**, **46**

libraries, in camps, **26**, 27

mail, of POWs, 18, 22-23, **40**

Moosburg, Germany, prison camp, 42

Nazi activity in camps, 41

newspapers, in camps, 16, **27**

number of POWs in war, **10**, 35, 45

Philippines, 7-9, **17**

plays, musicals in camps, 24, **24**, **25**

Polish prisoners of war, 12

radios, in POW camps, 23, **23**

radio stations, in POW camps, **26**

Russian prisoners of war, 12, **12**, 35, **42**, **43**, 45

Sagan prison camp, **24**, **25**, **26**, 30-34, **32**, **33**

Santo Tomas prison camp, **17**

Singapore, 14
South Africa, 28
Soviet Union, 13, 35, **35**
sports, in camps, **26**, 27, **36**
Stalag Luft 3, **24**, **25**
Stalin, Josef, 35
Stars and Stripes, **27**
starvation, in camps, 7, **9**, **12**, 15, **15**,
   19, **19**, 20

Switzerland, 13, 20, **20**
Thailand, 14
Trojan Horse Operation, 30-31
tunneling, out of camps, 30-34, **31**, **32**,
   33
uneven treatment of POWs, **10**, 11-12,
   45
Wainwright, Jonathan, 23
The Wooden Horse, 31

About the Author

Mr. Stein was born and grew up in Chicago. At eighteen he enlisted in the Marine Corps where he served three years. He was a sergeant at discharge. He later received a B.A. in history from the University of Illinois and an M.F.A. from the University of Guanajuato in Mexico.

Although he served in the Marines, Mr. Stein believes that wars are a dreadful waste of human life. He agrees with a statement once uttered by Benjamin Franklin: "There never was a good war or a bad peace." But wars are all too much a part of human history. Mr. Stein hopes that some day there will be no more wars to write about.